T0078397

MORNING'S CURTAIN

POEMS TO INSPIRE YOUR SOUL

MICHAEL SPENCE

WESTBOW
PRESS®
A DIVISION OF THOMAS NELSON
& ZONDERVAN

WestBow Press books may be ordered through booksellers or by contacting:

WestBow Press
A Division of Thomas Nelson & Zondervan
1663 Liberty Drive
Bloomington, IN 47403
www.westbowpress.com
844-714-3454

Cover design by Michael Verucchi

ISBN: 978-1-6642-1480-4 (sc)
ISBN: 978-1-6642-1479-8 (hc)
ISBN: 978-1-6642-1481-1 (e)

Library of Congress Control Number: 2020923671

Print information available on the last page.

WestBow Press rev. date: 01/14/2021

For Briana

and our three sons,
Luke, Ethan, and Weston.

For them I write …

"Many roads you will travel
As you progress on life's way

Follow your bliss, be your own author
Treat yourself kindly, be Brave!"

- Author

CONTENTS

Introduction ix

Chapter 1 **Poems of Hope** 1

I Am ... Hope 3
As We Move into April...................................5
This Tide Will Turn 6
A Storm Is a Chance 8
Never Quarantine Your Dreams........................ 10
October Surprise.. 12
Time Is Now... 14
Fear Not 16
Listen... 18
One Tear's Fall 20

Chapter 2 **Poems of Awe**....................................23

Morning's Curtain..25
How Numinous Is Our Universe 26
Never-Ending Friend......................................28
Dreams of Sailing 30
Storm Is a Dance 31
The GOAT..33
Paradise...35
Blessings..37
The Butterfly..39

Chapter 3 **Poems of Endearment** 41

By The Sea ... On Bended Knee 43
A Permanent Refrain......................................44
She Rides...46
Joy So Complete..48
Little Black Bird...49

Chapter 4   **Poems of Family**............................**51**

                Stand Up For Our Fathers.....................53
                We Are Dads.....................................55
                We Are Moms 57
                Our Home...59
                My Son 60

Chapter 5   **Poems of Reverence** **63**

                We Died For You 65
                Christmas Magic We Create.................68
                Roll Back Our Stone...........................70
                Our Bridge to the Father 72
                Larger Table of Our Hearts 74
                Where Were You 76
                Two and Forty Four 78

Chapter 6   **Poems of Riddles** ....**81 to 93**

Answers to Riddles **95**
About the Author **97**

INTRODUCTION

Five key themes resonate throughout this book of poems: Hope, Awe, Love, Family, Reverence. Underpinning every poem is the love God has for us, and the beauty He creates in and around us.

Hope. Often, we allow fear and anxiety to creep into our lives. They rob us of light and joy, and injure the spirit. During difficult times, whether a worldwide pandemic, political uncertainty, individual persecution, illness, the unbearable loss of a loved one, or just the emptiness we sometimes feel from the everyday tedium of life, Hope is, and will always remain, a salve for our soul, reminding us that all will be well again.

Awe. The magnificence of God's creation and His purpose can be found everywhere in nature; everyday, seen and unseen. A million examples exist all around us: the rise of the morning sun, the numinous stars in the night sky, the ever present companion of the moon, a rainbow bridging the horizon, a single butterfly passing in flight, the majesty of individual excellence.

Love and Family. The love we share with one another is a reflection of God's love for us, whether expressed in a passionate embrace, a tender interaction with nature, the feelings we have for our pets, the empathy we feel for a loved one's afflictions, and the affections we have for our family, friends, and neighbors, and much more.

Reverence. We celebrate special days and occasions as acts of reverence for the past, the present, and as security for our future. We honor them as expressions of faith, and to memorialize those who paid the ultimate price on our behalf to secure our freedoms. They are glue that binds us together as a community and humanity.

I would like to offer you my gratitude for purchasing this book and taking the time to read my poems. I sincerely believe this collection of poems will give you as much joy as they did when I wrote them. My hope is they will lift your spirit high, and leave your soul feeling renewed and invigorated. Enjoy.

Michael Spence
Memphis, TN

POEMS of HOPE

I AM ... HOPE

In those darkest of hours
When all appears broken
I show up to remind
Of life's beautiful moments.

Take a good look around
At all you can see—
New flowers in bloom,
Children at play and smiling.

I am wind and rain in your face,
Birds singing in tune.
Best prize of them all,
A rainbow in late afternoon.

My motto is never give up
And never give in.
It will be much better one day,
A promise you can depend.

May not happen today
Nor even tomorrow,
But joy will arrive, so
Rest easy, my dear fellow.

Starts as a whisper in your ear,
A beat in your heart,
Grows rapidly from there to
Give your dreams a jump start.

Whenever you feel lonely,
Defeated, or distressed
Breathe slowly, close your eyes,
And remember who has this.

I will never let you down;
I will never let you go.
It is said I'm spring eternal
And remain yours truly,

Hope.

AS WE MOVE INTO APRIL

As we move into April
And contagion rises high,
Stay away from close contact;
Let us turn this deadly tide.

As we move into April
With economic fears running deep,
Remember your neighbors
As they hurt and they weep.

As we move into April,
Do not be dismayed.
Embrace uncertainty with courage
And watch your fears fade away.

As we move into April
And rain showers resume,
Breathe in flowers around you
As they burst into bloom.

As we move into April
Celebrating the cross and His rise,
Ignite your passion for faith
For the Savior is alive.

As we move into April,
Keep your heads and your wits,
For again America will rise
With renewed greatness and grit!

THIS TIDE WILL TURN

—⚬⚬⚬—

2020 started so bright
With high hopes, stronger yearnings,
As a leap year to always remember,
An overflow of possibilities, and new beginnings.

January saw nothing amiss—
Markets rose high, ever higher,
Prosperity in abundance.
Reflecting a confidence like no other.

As cupid signaled his approach,
Markets rocketed farther above,
Oblivious to a pandemic offshore.
Soon a test of a country's resolve.

Winter gave way to spring;
Markets collapsed in unison.
Beware the ides of March—
Foretelling meteoric rise and ruination.

May flowers bloom so beautifully;
Economy in disarray and shambles.
Americans remain ever fearful.
Social distancing is the new preamble.

Summer comes never too soon.
A nation mourns heavy losses.
At last the tide is turning;
Contagion recedes as promised.

Youth return to their schools;
Nation's recovery now in sight.
Worst has fallen behind us.
Conquering this viral fright.

Fall leaves change so brightly;
Economy moves up the V-shaped curve.
Election looms before us,
Giving us leadership we all deserve.

Celebration of His birth is at hand
After a Thanksgiving to always remember.
Breaking bread with families and friends;
Grateful for our blessings and one another.

January 1 we start over again—
Bringing new change and greater purpose,
Moving forward with bold determination, and
Forever reflecting on the year that left us.

A STORM IS A CHANCE

What a day, what a day,
This is turning to be.
The kind that brings
Endless serenity.

Clouds are forming,
All willowy and white,
And the sun is shining
With intensity and delight.

Yet off in the distance
Clouds gather apace;
Their color turns dark.
A hidden menace awaits.

A storm is coming—
In fact, already here—
To bring ruin to our day
That started so pure.

It comes rolling and rolling
And rolling our way,
Marching to the tune
Of chaos and decay.

The day turns dark,
Air cackles with fright,
As lights burst above
And thunder roars its might.

The sky opens up and
Rain pours like a fount,
Increasing its flow
With each passing moment.

As we bend and cower
From the onslaught above,
A thought comes to mind
Of clarity and wisdom.

An opportunity is shown
Within every storm and crisis,
A silver lining, some call it,
To confront even a deadly virus.

Storm lights and thunder
Are not always meant for harm.
They can be God's way of showing
Humanity's love should be affirmed.

A storm is a chance,
Often not realized till it is over,
To lay aside our deepest fears
And help our brothers and our neighbors.

NEVER QUARANTINE YOUR DREAMS

Class of 2020,
Your time has finally arrived.
Many years of hard study—
You did it! You survived!

As you conjure your future
Asking what this now means,
One thing you must remember is to
Never quarantine your dreams!

They are not meant to be shelved
Nor kept out of sight
But nourished with courage.
They will always take flight.

Like those who came before,
Take your future by storm.
Live each day to the full;
Grab that bull by its horns.

Your birthright is not retreat;
It is not six feet away.
Not locked in your homes
Or asked to play another day.

It is not wearing a mask
That fits always too tight;
It is not curbside service
All day and the night.

This time is now yours to
Prove naysayers wrong.
Remember your birthright and
Dream big! Dream on!

Many roads you will travel
As you progress on life's way.
Follow your bliss, be your own author,
Treat yourself kindly, and be brave!

Graduates of 2020
Of every school color and hue,
Be the promise for a better tomorrow—
Our nation is counting on you!

OCTOBER SURPRISE

October ... October,
A month like no other,
Where we expect the unexpected,
Unlike the constancy of summer.

A fresh cool is in the air.
Breathe it in ... breathe it in.
Wreaths bloom on doors everywhere,
Foretelling of change to begin.

Trees wearing their disguises:
Shades of orange, red, brown and more.
As autumn tells us she is ready
For her symphony of color to adore.

Spells of summer dreams are broken,
Replaced by fall's bountiful charm.
To orchestrate with precision
A world of new to regard.

Fear not ... Fear not.
Embrace with less alarm and more vigor.
We're not meant to live in permanence;
Growth comes only from the irregular.

What makes October surprises special,
For Libras and all the rest,
Has nothing to do with politics
As I'm sure you can all attest.

Don't look for the election to give you
The change you think you need.
It can come only from within
And the October choices that you feed.

TIME IS NOW

Our lives are short.
You've heard it before.
Here for a moment,
Then gone like a vapor.

You wake up one morning
With eyes opened wide,
Reflecting on your life
And the years flown by.

Where did the time go?
You keep asking yourself.
How did it get away,
And out of your control?

Is there something you wish
To do more than ever?
Something you once had imagined
That time could not capture?

A book to be written,
An instrument to be played,
A race to be won, or
An obstacle to negotiate?

A mountain to climb,
Perhaps even an Everest,
A boat to sail solo
Around a Cape's often treacherous?

A new career to start fresh
In the middle of your life;
A passion not a job and
One you can monetize?

A fork in the road
To cross without doubt.
A new path to travel,
Avoiding the easy and safer routes?

It is never too late.
You know the drill.
Yet very well could be,
As time never stands still.

So go find your dreams,
Up there on the shelf.
Take them down, brush them off,
And rediscover yourself.

Your life is not over
In fact, it's just started.
Be the dreamer of your youth, and
A new course you'll have charted.

FEAR NOT

———— ∞∞∞ ————

Creeps up out of nowhere,
When you're feeling your best.
Never invited to any table,
Much less honored as favored guest.

Yet it lingers and lingers,
Growing larger by the second,
Blocking out all the light,
And with it all enjoyment.

Found everywhere you are,
And just beneath the surface.
It hides just out of sight
To defeat your every purpose.

On that stage when you're alone
To give your practiced performance.
At the end of an election when
Our country's path remains uncertain.

Shadow over your heart, before
Your loved one passes away.
The other whisper in your ear
When you've lost your will to pray.

It pushes you back to the edge just
When you think you've turned a corner.
A pandemic's closest friend,
Feeding off one another.

Can be defeated with some permanence,
But requires close attention.
Just have to say the word, and
Its power over you is broken.

But courage it will take
To remove it from your life, and
The firm conviction within you
That Hope will never die.

LISTEN

Listen.
Listen
To their pleas and protestations
From generation to generation.
Seeds sown of mistrust and suspicion.

Listen.
Listen
To the sound of gunfire in the city.
Mothers forced to grieve too soon as
Sons killed in a continuum of tragedy.

Listen.
Listen
To brave officers in shield and blue,
Who daily risk their lives
To protect and serve me and you.

Listen.
Listen.
They are every race and color,
Always home late to see their children
Who love them like any other.

Listen.
Listen.
A black man tragically lost his life
Under the knee of a crooked cop,
But do not assume all police are alike.

Listen.
Listen.
Truth rings unanimous.
Justice should always be blind of color, but
Her light dims from destruction and chaos.

Listen.
Listen.
Achieving progress takes courageous stands.
Let's make his dream a reality from
The mountaintop to the Promised Land.

ONE TEAR'S FALL

One tear's fall
Touches my soul,
Reminding me how fragile
Life is to behold.

One tear's fall
Tells a story complete,
Breathing life to a daughter's
Beautiful memories.

One tear's fall
For my own contemplation,
Encouraging I live faithfully
And without exception.

One tear's fall
Reminds me never to forget.
She was beautifully made
Like a rose's blooming silhouette.

One tear's fall
Touches my soul.
God knows of my sorrows,
And will never let me go.

One tear's fall
Brings me quickly to my knees.
Obedient to His promise,
I'll see her again in Eternity.

Where she'll be adorned in a white robe,
Playing ivory keys at His feet,
A choir of angels all around,
To make His orchestra complete.

God's love is in the tear,
Falling down my Claire's cheek.
Miraculously giving me the
Comfort that I seek.

* Inspired by a mother's sorrow from the sudden, tragic loss of her vibrant, musically gifted, 14 year old daughter, Claire Elizabeth, to HUS, caused by an Ecoli 0157 food borne illness, and her steadfast hope of seeing Claire again in Heaven.

POEMS OF AWE

MORNING'S CURTAIN

With glorious waves of sunlight
Bursting through the veil,

Proclaimer of new beginnings,
She extends her reach to all.

Oh, peace.
Oh, joy.
Colors of bliss made to dazzle.

Oh, majesty.
Oh, eminence.
God's glory, indescribable.

Can you see it?
Diamonds dancing on the surface.

Can you feel it?
Warm vibrations in the distance.

As endless waves kiss the shoreline
Leaving me hypnotic in my state,

Thoughts of wonder overwhelm me,
Reminding of His grace.

His presence is felt everywhere,
Of that you can be certain.

But nowhere more revealed
Than the rise of morning's curtain.

HOW NUMINOUS IS OUR UNIVERSE

Have you ever gazed deep,
So deep into the sky,
And asked yourself a question
Over and over again, Why?

Why this blue rock
We love to call our Earth
Is third in the planetary line-up
And not even the first?

Why 93 million miles
In loose change, give or take,
Separates our Earth from the sun,
A divine calculus made too vague?

Why does the sun burn so bright
In hues of yellow, not red or blue,
As it travels across the sky
To set in wonder for me and you?

Why the number of all the stars
Seen at night from any distance
Is like a single drop of water
In the ocean's vast magnificence?

What is the total sum of stars
In the universe? No one knows.
Can you put your arms around infinity
Or conjure a one preceding eighteen zeros?

Why are our sun and planetary sisters
Found midway up the spiraling arm,
Not the center of the Milky Way Galaxy
Where you'd think we should all belong?

Is this just random, or
Is this simply chance that
We are neither in the center nor the
Focus of this celestial dance?

Or is this God's way of teaching us
Through cosmic chaos and seeming futility
That there is purpose to His design, prescribing
Far less pride and much more humility?

NEVER-ENDING FRIEND

Steadfast in the heavens
Before time began,
It is always on the move—
A never-ending friend.

Its light leads the way
For ships under duress;
Its multitude of color reminds of
Seasons to plant and harvest.

The ancients gave it names
For the gods they most liked.
They alone knew the meaning
Of its all-consuming light.

Even the oceans bow
To its ability to warp and bend
As the tides ebb and flow
To its ever-changing whim.

Competes with the sun and stars
For every story told,
But the poet knows it best
For lovers young and old.

No less, its power and eminence
Is something we can all relate—
Strolling the beach with your love
Under its soft and luminous gaze.

Though humanity may disagree
On issues large to very small,
It is marvelous to know its moonlight
Binds and connects us all.

DREAMS OF SAILING

Oh, how I love the feel
Of waves crashing against her bow
When she dances with the ocean
At twenty knots or more.

Wind is always a friend,
A companion you most treasure.
It fills your sails generously
As its power thrusts you forward.

Sea is my muse,
Spinning spells through the night
To destinations unknown
By the moon's beautifying light.

Pleasure unrivaled
Is how I can only describe
Yet a thousand times more
With your beloved by your side.

STORM IS A DANCE

What a day, what a day,
This is turning to be.
The kind that brings
Endless serenity.

Clouds are forming
All willowy and white,
And the sun is shining
With intensity and delight.

Far off in the distance
Clouds are gathering apace;
Their color turns dark
And menace awaits.

A storm is coming—
Of that I am sure—
To bring ruin to my day
That started so pure.

They come rolling and rolling
And rolling my way,
Marching to the tune
Of chaos and decay.

Day becomes dark
Air cackles with fright,
As lights burst above
And thunder roars its might.

The sky opens up, and
Rain pours like a fount,
Increasing its flow
With each passing moment.

As I begin to cower
From the onslaught above,
A thought pierces my mind
Of clarity and wisdom.

The light and the thunder
Are not meant to harm,
For it is God's way of showing
Life's beauty and charm.

A Storm is a Dance,
An expression of God's pleasure.
So, lay down your fears
And embrace it with wonder.

THE GOAT

Coming on to the scene
Like a well-heeled fellow,
Then a bull set loose
A new generation's virtuoso.

No one like him now,
No one like him before,
No one like him since,
Neither outplayed nor outscored.

Not a Bird in the garden
Nor a Magic alone,
Could equal his prowess
Or cast him from his throne.

He took off in the air,
Soles ablaze in the sky.
Made it look all too easy,
As he climbed way up high.

For many a year
He negotiated that slump.
Took the Bad Boys defeat
To get over the hump.

Then six wins in eight,
As history will say.
Eight for eight for sure,
Had he not retired that day.

There can be no doubt, he's
The Greatest Of All Time.
All due respect to the other,
But thinking differently is a crime.

PARADISE

Alone at your desk, or
In the car with your kids,
Any time of the day, and
Anywhere on life's grid.

A trickle of a thought,
Quickly picking up steam,
Anchors body and soul,
Before setting sail as a dream.

Yes, the dream we all dream
When our minds need a rest;
A far away place of
Complete harmony and happiness.

An island in the Pacific and
Crystalline waters of azure blue.
Palm trees all around, with
White sand polishing the dunes.

Walking among the cypress
In the hills above Tuscany.
Strolling cobblestone streets amid
Alabaster spells of Santorini.

On the top of that mountain,
Where the air is crisp and clear,
Breathing new life to a spirit
That's numbed over the years.

Perhaps nearer to home
Is that place you dream most,
Like the joy in your teen's face,
You feared would always be lost.

Your island and your mountain
Need not be a far off place.
If they reside in your heart,
You need never give them chase.

Not quite the same from
One person to the next, but
Depends solely on you and
How you imagine life's best.

BLESSINGS

Touch football at twilight.
Whipped cream in hot coco.
Rocky road ice cream.
Caramel and marshmallows.

A spoonful of icing,
when no one is looking.
The aroma of sunshine and
Mom's wholesome cooking.

Lazy afternoon naps,
That never finish too soon.
Lone sparrow on your window,
Whistling in tune.

Catching raindrops on your tongue,
Like you did when you were young.
And those tickle tackle wars,
Creating perpetual fun.

Dreaming of that rainbow,
Just out of reach,
Tracing its curve with your eyes and
Letting your imagination unleash.

As you make it to the top,
Looking out across the land, and
Wondering from where does it start,
And does it have an end.

Your blessings are alive and
Everywhere you can see.
Like the view from your rainbow,
They are never ending.

THE BUTTERFLY

I move here and there
All the days of my life.
You may not see me coming,
Much less hear when I arrive.

Unlike birds of the sky,
Who always sing in tune,
I move always in silence
And often alone.

I touch down for a moment,
As a brief whispered hello,
Then take off with the wind
To a destination unknown.

I start life with a crawl,
And keep crawling away.
Who could ever believe,
What I would become one day.

After weeks and weeks
Of climbing that tree,
Something strange and magical
Happens to me.

Where once I was average,
And even much less,
God singles me out
To be the top of life's best.

Known over the world
Along with flowers of summer,
My wings are my petals
And they bloom like no other.

You may think you are average, and
Not worthy of advance,
But He has designs for your life,
If you just give Him a chance.

The change you are seeking
Is well within reach.
Believe first in yourself and
Your potential He will unleash.

You will not sprout wings
In a colorful array,
But the beauty inside you
Will grow magnificent one day.

POEMS of ENDEARMENT

BY THE SEA ... ON BENDED KNEE

It is true what is said,
Said about the sea.
That the sea is for lovers—
One on bended knee.

You know what I mean.
It is how the sea draws you in.
Breathes new life to your soul,
Elevating passion over reason.

It is a walk in the sand,
A tingle between your toes.
Taking your love's hand,
And never letting go.

It is waves rolling in,
Kissing the beach with each rise,
Then rolling out again,
Sent to tease and tantalize.

A deep blue of mystery,
Gives way to white crests of meaning,
Conveying one's love for the other—
Souls forever connecting.

So remember this well
As you take your amorous leap,
The sea is for lovers—
A promise forever to keep.

A PERMANENT REFRAIN

A Poet knows,
Knows the source of his inspiration—
A longing for his Love
Through skillful expression.

He never strings mere words,
Together for the multiplicity.
His words are strung for her
And for her alone to see.

He paints with his words,
Brush strokes of finesse—
An unrestrained passion
Put to imaginary canvass.

Poetry is wild.
Unruly, as a Pollock or van Gogh,
As divine and sublime,
As a Raphael or Leonardo.

It is without rules or restraints
And hers to keep.
To drink to her fill
As with an aged whiskey.

Need not make her think,
Laugh or cry.
Need not win her heart,
Touch her soul or mystify.

A simple smile on her face will do.
But one that lingers there, enduring—
As a permanent refrain.
That is his longing.

SHE RIDES

She rides.
She rides,
Like a comet from the sky.

On her magnificent black steed,
Effortlessly, they glide.

She is beauty.
She is light.
She is imagination supreme.

She is gaiety.
She is freedom.
She is the essence of our dreams.

With uncanny precision
She rides without fear.

Like Epona divine,
She rides with grandeur.

No man can catch her,
Though many have tried.

Her steed is too swift,
Casting mere mortals aside.

No man can claim her,
As she rides with the wind,

Forsaking all before her,
But her dreams and her whims.

Her steed is her Love;
A friendship reassuring.

Together they ride,
Forever enduring.

JOY SO COMPLETE

Nothing in this world quite compares
To his unfathomable love, I declare.

His piercing gaze with deep brown eyes
Never fails to allure or mesmerize.

Even the most ardent feline friend
Cannot resist his charm's intend.

But faithful is his love I say
As he leaves my side, ne'er for a day.

Through calm or stormy nights persist,
His furled presence, I cannot resist.

He brings me joy so complete
As he rests his head at my feet.

And at times I may be far away
To rest my soul near ocean's waves.

I know for certain where he stands—
Firmly in my thoughts without end.

What is his name, you ask, unsure?
Well, that is an easy one to share.

Come here Knoxy! … Come here boy!

LITTLE BLACK BIRD

Little black bird
Fell from the sky
And landed with a thump
Just inches nearby.

I quickly ran to it
To see for myself
Why little black bird
Would lay there and yelp.

With soft textured hands
And a mother's keen care,
I picked up little black bird
And whispered in its ear.

As I caressed its feathers,
It looked up at me, and
I swore at that moment
I saw it smile with glee.

To my utter surprise,
And joyous delight,
My little black bird
Flew off into the night.

Often, I wonder
About the fragility of life,
Of an infant's tears
And a brief kiss goodnight.

From little black bird
A lesson suggests—
God's love even extends to the
Smallest and tenderest of us.

POEMS of FAMILY

STAND UP FOR OUR FATHERS

Stand up for our fathers,
Born midst famine and war,
Leaving family and home
When country needed them more.

Stand up for our fathers,
Our heroes when we were young,
Sitting snuggly in their laps,
Hearing stories being spun.

Stand up for our fathers,
Living through upheaval and strife,
Equipped with little understanding, yet
Forced to adapt to this new life.

Stand up for our fathers,
Who sacrificed much to see us grow,
Working long days with calloused hands
With little in gratitude to show.

Stand up for our fathers,
Some falling to deep despair,
With no one to talk to
And too proud to share.

Stand up for our fathers,
Show them forgiveness less shame,
For no one can really know
The true depth of their pain.

These fathers for whom we stand
Now 80 years and greater,
Embrace them with love
For they need us more than ever.

And a word of advice
For us fathers coming later,
Give honor to those men,
Who sacrificed much in our favor.

WE ARE DADS

Coached your teams in your youth,
Baseball, basketball and more.
Could little contain my joy,
As you played with intensity and vigor.

Read you stories of heroes
Late into the night.
Watched in magnificent wonder
As your imagination took flight.

Had tickle tackle wars,
Leaving us weary and battle scarred.
Tears streaming down our faces
As we laughed together so hard.

Watched you wrap yourself in sadness
Over the end of a romance.
Encouraged you never to feel defeated—
To always give love another chance.

Wiped a tear from your face
When you were bullied at school.
Taught you to always stand firm
When they came looking for you.

Had that talk that we needed.
You know the one.
That made you giggle and giggle—
A serious talk turned to fun.

Prayed over and over you
Long into the night.
Prayed the Lord would protect you
From sin and evil's plight.

As I remind you again,
And again and again,
My number one job
Is to protect your heart from sin.

To teach you right from wrong,
To win and to lose,
To make difficult choices,
To make fewer excuses.

To stand up for your beliefs
And your neighbor's too.
Know I will always be your champion
And that I will always love you.

WE ARE MOMS

She was right there in the beginning,
As you tossed and turned inside,
Right there in the beginning,
When you entered with eyes open wide.

Hers was the first song you heard,
Deep inside her womb.
Hers was the first kiss you felt,
As you lay beside her bosom.

She was first to hold you close,
The night your fever hit 103.
Would not leave your side for a second,
Even when the heat finally broke free.

She did everything for her children—
Teach, cook, pray, set curfew.
Repeat … everything for her children,
Sacrificing career advancement too.

The real head of every household,
As a wise man and husband knows.
She is the life blood of her family—
A son and daughter's first hero.

Her love will never waiver, even
If you are a thousand miles away,
And comes without condition,
As she has proven time and time again.

It is so right we celebrate our Mothers
On this single day in May.
But need to celebrate them more often,
Like every hour of every day.

OUR HOME

That place, where we …

Rest our weary heads,
Calm our fears of dread,

Raise our family new,
Grow it two by two,

Welcome holiday gatherings,
Celebrate our hopes and dreams,

Sit at the table in harmony, to
Savor a good morning's coffee,

Rest from a hard day's labor,
Cherish friendships with neighbors,

Listen to Susie's piano,
Practice Billy's baseball throw,

Find comfort as the norm,
Shelter from rain and storm,

Pray for bountiful blessings,
Be grateful for God's bestowing's.

Home resides first in our hearts,
The place where Love first gathers and starts,

Yet so much more,
Since we take it wherever we go.

MY SON

My son.
My son.
You make your parents proud,
First among your brothers,
Leader in a crowd.

My son.
My son.
Your smile's a contagion,
Among your friends and family,
Spreading joy and affection.

My son.
My son.
You light up our lives;
A neutron bomb of energy,
Bursting through your eyes.

My son.
My son.
Your love gives us hope,
Keep your eyes on the ball, and
Your Faith never let go.

My son.
My son.
Keep growing in your knowledge,
Since the years are getting closer
When we will send you off to college.

My son.
My son.
You turned twelve years today—
Proof time never stands still,
Nor will it ever be contained.

My son.
My son.
Our turn to celebrate you—
Have a wonderful time
And happiest of Birthdays Luke!

POEMS of REVERENCE

WE DIED FOR YOU

———— ∞∞ ————

Young men from the farms,
City streets and small towns,
From all over the land, we
Left our families and homes.

No different from you, with
Abundant dreams and whims.
With many hearts to lose,
But only one heart to win.

We followed that Flag,
When it tugged on our hearts—
A call from our country
To do our small part.

Our differences shattered,
In the foxholes we shared.
Becoming brothers in battle,
To face together our fears.

On island shores in the Pacific
And French beaches in June,
From Belleau Wood to the Bulge,
Our blood spilled on distant ruins.

We are found row upon row,
As far as your eyes can see,
Over fields of white crosses—
Two unknown, perhaps more than three.

You see freedom is not free,
For it comes at a steep price—
Our lives for yours,
To live free of sacrifice.

We thank you for this honor
On this last Monday in May,
To remember sons and daughters;
A nation's chance to repay.

For the millions like us,
Whose lives were cut short
In the flower of our youth,
So your freedoms can endure.

Mark Fisher, a young lieutenant junior grade (LTJG) in
the United States Coast Guard, lost his life *for us* in 1993,
while undertaking helicopter maneuvers. His legacy lives
on through his son and daughter, now grown with families
of their own.

CHRISTMAS MAGIC WE CREATE

Boy, aged 9, at St Jude
Hears he is finally cancer free.
Many prayers were said for him
By mere strangers, like you and me.

Bright lights on the family tree
Dimmed for years from parental wrongs.
Took the children's fervent wishes and
Love's spark to turn them on.

Old war veteran alone at home.
All he loved either dead or gone.
Neighbor stops by his house to share
Warm soup and some conversation.

Homeless man down on his luck
On the corner of Kirby and 385.
You drive to him with some lunch and
Warm clothes to survive the night.

Close friendship for many years,
Broken from mistrust and things said.
You pick up your phone to call, only to
Find how much you've missed your friend.

The magic of Christmas is not
Santa on his sleigh,
the Elf on his shelf, or
Outside lights we've on display.

It is the inexplicable joy
We feel inside for no other reason,
Than to show love for our fellow man
In his neediest of seasons.

It comes over us like a rush,
And most often this time of year,
As we prepare for His birth,
Sharing our joy and good cheer.

ROLL BACK OUR STONE

Who were we?
Just men performing our duty
Our lives forever altered,
When He brought us into His story.

Before then our days were simple,
Awakened well before the dawn,
Trained as soldiers in the army
With far less heart than brawn.

We were young and unattached.
Our devotion to Empire complete.
But that day changed us forever,
Soldiers now to worship at His feet.

We were first to see the Miracle
On that fateful Sunday morn, that
Changed humanity's trajectory—
Lost to sin, risen to be found.

He brings each of us into His story
When we roll back our stone.
Makes an ordinary life, extra, and
The unknown life, known.

But His Gift is never forced;
A decision His only request.
To follow Him forever, and
Be faithful to your breath's last.

Who were we again?
Our answer may surprise.
We were the Guards who fell asleep
By that stone with Him inside.

OUR BRIDGE TO THE FATHER

A long time ago, in the
Stillness of the night, a
Child was born under
A star's mystifying light.

Throughout the land of Judah
The good news quickly spread,
Proclaiming a new King's beginning,
Confirming old King Herod's dread.

With His unassuming entry,
The narrative began to change.
As the Prophets had foretold,
The world would never be the same.

Before arriving on the scene,
Sin held the upper hand,
Keeping the Father at a distance;
A spiritual death for all Men.

He came into this world
To be the One like no other;
A beacon of living hope and
Our only bridge to the Father.

His coming fulfilled the Law,
Given by Moses to the Hebrew nation,
Allowing grace to be all you need
To receive the gift of eternal salvation.

So on this Christmas Day, As we
celebrate the birth of our Lord,
Remember the meaning behind it
And endeavor not to ignore.

Giving gifts is a marvelous expression,
We use this day to share our love.
But the greatest gift, Wonderful Counselor,
Came to us first from His Father above.

LARGER TABLE OF OUR HEARTS

For your brother, your sister,
Your mother, your father.
For your son, your daughter,
Your friend, your neighbor.

As I sit at your table,
Bringing blessings and good cheer,
I make room for a larger table
In the hearts of many this time of year.

An invitation to streets of sadness,
For those in midst of distress,
Where no joy exists,
Only supreme loneliness.

To the hungry little orphan,
Without a family to call her own.
To the widow in her twilight,
With only her memories to bemoan.

To the son grieving in pain,
For a father recently passed.
To the teen caught up in crime,
Without a parent to guide her path.

To the unemployed veteran,
Who served his country right.
To the child escaping poverty
In the dead cold of night.

To the mother fighting illness
From cancer's unrelenting rage.
To the grandparent in a nursing home,
Forced to cope alone in old age.

Thanksgiving should have a meaning
Far greater than our own;
An invitation to a larger table for Humanity's
lost and suffering souls.

So on this happy day,
Filled rightly with love and gratitude,
May we take a few moments to pray
For the far less fortunate multitude.

WHERE WERE YOU

Where were you the day
Our lives changed forever?
Where were you the day
Heroes arose from nowhere?

Where were you the day
Our children grieved for their parents?
Where were you the day
Innocence was lost to circumstance?

Where were you the day
Our tallest turned to dust?
Where were you the day
Shattered was our trust?

Where were you the day
Our friends and families cried?
Where were you the day
The best of us tried and died?

Where were you the day
Our country came together?
Where were you the day
We joined hands to pray with strangers?

Where were you the day
The mighty fell by a few's warped justice?
Where were you the day
The many responded with virtuous sacrifice?

Like you, I know exactly where I was
That grievous September day,
On my way to work where I
Dropped on my knees to pray.

Our country had been attacked.
Thousands upon thousands had died;
Futures destroyed and families shattered
In a mere instant of time.

Our country owes an eternal debt of gratitude to those
brave men and women who answered the call of duty
without hesitation on that fateful day nearly 20 years ago:
First responders, flight 93 passengers, hospital personnel
and the servicemen and women who fought the resultant
wars in Afghanistan and Iraq

TWO AND FORTY FOUR

Two and Forty Four,
To you what does it mean?
The birthing of a nation,
Unlike any the world has seen.

Two and Forty Four,
To you what does it mean?
Fifty six men coming together,
Declaring All men equal and free.

Two and Forty Four,
To you what does it mean?
Not all men were considered equal—
Moral contrast, fated to bring calamity.

Two and Forty Four,
To you what does it mean?
Bursting lights high in the sky—
Beacon to millions chasing a dream.

Two and Forty Four
To you what does it mean?
Never take our Freedoms for granted.
Protect them well for next generations to see.

Two and Forty Four,
To me what this day means?
My sons can grow up knowing
They can be who they wish to be.

Ours is the only nation on earth
Where circumstance of birth has no claim.
You are not anchored to your past
Nor guaranteed a future based on surname.

Ours is the only nation on earth
When its Promises come up short,
Never fails to correct its wrongs
Always ready to right its course.

Wherever you fall on the political spectrum take a moment to reflect what brings us together; this day in July 244 years ago when a document was signed creating the greatest force for Freedom the world has ever known. Our nation was deeply flawed in its beginning and for many decades after. But we continue to be the World's and Humanity's Best Hope of that I am certain.

POEMS OF RIDDLES

See Page (95) for Answers to Riddles

WHAT AM I?

By your side when you were born,
A handy friend when you mourned.

Your neighbors knew me well enough.
Unpleasantly surprised when they woke up.

Silky smooth to feel and touch.
But not always, you have known as much.

At the bottom, valued never best,
Only to rise high during periods of unrest.

Butt of every joke these past days,
Behind the meltdown and viral craze.

Hoard me well or suffer consequence,
Unloading your burden without proper defense.

Try not to worry,
Try not to rush,
Though I may not be there when you flush.

Why is this riddle so ridiculous and inane.
Should everything I write be sublime and arcane?

WHAT AM I?

All over
The strip, and
Hungry for
More chips.

Whether tossed
Or passed,
There is never
Going back.

Every game
I play a role;
Move forward
Or lose control.

Some have the lot,
Others mere cry,
Where I will fall
Always governs why.

Some sink
Into trouble
With me
And my double.

Others throw me
To the wall,
Numbers summed,
Wins it all.

So remember well,
My dear friend,
Like throwing caution
To the wind,

Your future
Always will rest
On the figures
I manifest.

WHAT AM I?

—⊗⊗⊗—

I'm every gift imaginable,
Spreading joy for young and old.
But beyond gratuitous giving,
There is much more of me to be told.

I'm wholesome food on a table,
Not scraps on the floor to share.
Warm shelter from the elements,
Like the windy and frosty air.

I'm a brother and sister for her,
A family she has never known.
I'm reconciliation in their marriage,
Broken from years of love not shown.

I'm shared company in her twilight,
Knowing only loneliness and dread.
I'm forgiveness between father and son
For the many words gone unsaid.

I'm cure from long term illness
That ravages body and mind.
I'm inspiration for a young man,
Struggling for himself to find.

I'm the ending of ancient hostilities
Near the strip beyond the wall
I'm safe return to his family
From a war that still rages on.

I'm new shoes on thirteen-year-old Julio
Trekking north to escape his fears.
I'm the diamond on her finger,
Of which she has dreamt for many years.

Make no mistake about me
Your children know me well.
But as you can clearly see,
There is far more of me to tell.

WHAT AM I?

Sir Winston spoke of me
A long time ago,
About an enigmatic threat
On the rise from Moscow.

My meaning is shrouded
And never in one place.
Keep scratching your heads
For answers difficult to trace.

I am a staple of the courts
Where there is ambiguity to argue,
Leaving many of you stymied
In search of the next clue.

I keep many of you guessing,
My foremost distinction,
With Life's greatest questions,
As in our Savior's conception.

My talents go further
With inquiries that matter,
Like what came before us,
And is there a hereafter.

WHAT AM I?

——⊶⊶——

I come when it is cold,
And never alone.

I am considered quite rare, yet
More like others from afar.

Arriving quietly at your feet,
Early risers are who I seek.

I bring happiness to children's lives.
Just ask them to tell you why.

Shoulder to shoulder we all stand,
Bringing excitement to cover the land.

When their courage seems broke,
I become used as some jokes.

Trouble deciphering, this riddle?
Then put this to a scribble:

Think former Senators from the right—
In Maine she went home,
To Arizona he took flight.

WHAT AM I?

Come ride on my ship
As it sails away
To faraway lands
At midnight and a day.

I will show you places
You have never seen,
So take hold of my hand
And come with me.

I will take you up high,
Way up high in the sky,
Where you drift with the clouds
With your wings spread out wide.

We will soar through lush valleys,
To the top of the hills,
Then plummet straight downward
To touch summer's daffodils.

Be anyone you like
In this grand five act play.
Do anything you wish
Without fear or delay.

WHAT AM I?

—❦—

I hide in the darkness
Out of sight out of mind.
I step forward to the light,
Leaving all mystery behind.

I am needed the most
To keep enemies at bay,
But also by boys
And girls at play.

My reputation may depend
On the Godfather's wishes.
Give me up too soon, and
He'll have you swim with the fishes.

I am very well guarded
In some areas of life,
And will never be found out
In that cold beverage you like.

I am big.
I am little,
And even at the top.
And I will always be needed
As long as trust drops.

WHAT AM I?

—⚭—

I can be wet or dry,
And any color you like.

I leave a stain when disguised,
And can be made to surprise.

Only one is desired,
Though two is required.

Forever I am encased,
In Parisian marble with good taste.

Made famous in the camera's glare,
At war's end near Times Square.

Key role I did play
In His story at Gethsemane.

WHAT AM I?

It comes in waves
And never hesitates.

It changes color with the seasons,
For no other reason.

It smells of lush irresistible,
Oh, so delectable.

Its caress makes them blush,
No telling ... shhh!

It conforms to few rules, and is
A purveyor of cool

Its aim is to please ...
And to tease and tease and tease!

ANSWERS TO RIDDLES

1. Toilet Paper
2. Rolling Dice
3. Christmas Wish
4. Mystery
5. Snowflake
6. Mid-Summer's Night Dream
7. Secret
8. A Kiss
9. Woman's Hair

ABOUT THE AUTHOR

With roots in Texas, Michael Spence is a marketing executive who currently resides in the Memphis, TN, area with his wife, Briana, and three sons, Luke, Ethan, and Weston, ages 12, 11, and 10, respectively.

Morning's Curtain is his first publication of poetry. His next project, already in progress, is a short story titled, Roll Back Our Stone, a fictionalized account of the lives of two Roman soldiers who fell asleep guarding Christ's tomb. Publication will be 2021.

Printed in the United States
By Bookmasters